TREASURES
IN JARS OF CLAY

Written and Illustrated by
MICHELLE L. COLEMAN

Copyright © 2016 Written and Illustrated by Michelle L. Coleman

Treasures in Jars of Clay
Written and Illustrated by Michelle L. Coleman

Printed in the United States of America.

ISBN 9781498485814

All rights reserved solely by the author. The author guarantees all contents are original and do not infringe upon the legal rights of any other person or work. No part of this book may be reproduced in any form without the permission of the author. The views expressed in this book are not necessarily those of the publisher.

www.xulonpress.com

To our precious and gracious Heavenly Father Yahweh, there are no words to convey the love that I feel for you. It is because of you that I write. Your love must be made known to those who know you not. How can one accurately write about you? You are everything!

The beauty of your perfection and holiness defies description.

May you eternally remain most holy, most powerful and most sovereign forever and ever, and let it be so.

Yahshua, what a true blessing, and perfect gift you are. Our Heavenly Father is so blessed to have you as his only begotten son. Glory be to him for allowing you to be given to us. You are our life's blood and the very air that we breathe. I am eternally indebted to you. Thank you. Bless you my King. To you be wisdom and honor and blessing and power, forever and ever, and let it be so.

This book is dedicated to the heroes of Autism. Many of which reside in my own Family. To my husband Sylvester, you are my warrior angel with invisible wings. You embody courage strength and great wisdom. I stand in awe of the gifts that autism has given you. You are in no way limited by them. You instead have been empowered by them. I admire the man of God that you've become. I will love you forever. To my oldest Amber, you have been blessed with many gifts I look forward to seeing how they will continue to manifest in your life. You will go on to do great things, for greatness lives in you, I love you. To my two youngest, Zion and Amira. Thank you both for the hidden treasures that Autism brings. Though you both have the same diagnosis, it teaches in such different ways. You both are beautiful not in spite of Autism, but because of it. And last but not least, to my grandson Samuel, you my dear one, remind me so much of Zion when he was young. Your diagnosis completes the most blessed of gifts. You are exquisite in your childlike wonder. May you continue to blossom as beautifully as the butterfly as it breaks forth from its cocoon.

CONTENTS

1) Introduction 11
2) Diagnosis: the news No one Desires to hear 13
3) Innocent Until Proven Guilty 19
4) Picking up the Shattered Pieces 28
5) Divide and Conquer: The effects Of Autism on Marriage. 37
6.) Acceptance: Seeing Autism Through the Eyes of Truth 43
7) The Eyes of an Eagle 51
8) To Discipline or Not to Discipline 58
9) The Sum of All Fears 66
10) A Letter to Dads 75
11) A Letter to Moms 77
12) The Echo of Responsibility. 79
13) Treasures in Jars of Clay 88

SAIL

The waves they ride
Are the seas of life
The storms they brave
Forges character of might

The lessons they learn
Whether succeed or fail
Are navigated by Autism
As the heart doth sail

Michelle Coleman

Chapter 1

Introduction

So many are the plans that we have for our unborn children. As they lie in repose during the long awaited months of pregnancy, we begin to construct our fairy tale rendition of what WE would like their lives to be. There is an automatic assumption that our unborn children will prosper and be in good health. Our objective is to base all future plans on this supposition. From the planning of the nursery to the establishment of a future college fund, our aim is to navigate a well-adjusted child through this thing that we call life.

The long sojourn of pregnancy finally comes to an end. We are elated that this little bundle instantaneously inserts into our lives an unspeakable joy. And why not, for indeed that is what babies were meant to do. They bring such meaning and fulfillment to our lives that our intrinsic desire is to reciprocate the same to them. And so we strive to do all that we can to create a well-balanced and ideal living environment so as to give them EVERY opportunity to grow and become a well-rounded individual.

Then comes the day that our dreams come to a screeching halt. The day comes when we realize that our little bundle of joy has been high jacked by a sinister foe. Autism has taken captive the ones that we hold most dear. How do we come to terms with this most pervasive of diagnoses? How do we accept the fate of raising a child with this kind of challenge? And how do we keep firmly in our grasp the "normal" life that we desire this child to live?

Chapter 2

Diagnosis: The News no one Desires To Hear

P art of our role as parents is to keep close watch over the development of our children. We automatically keep track of their milestones: comparing their progress to the progress of their peers. In general, the progress report measures up, and all is right with the world. However, this is not the reality of the parents of children with Autism. Long before there is a diagnosis, there is the presumption that our children are healthy and that their cognitive development is on the same level as their peers. Although there is this presumption, there's also a nagging suspicion that something is not quite right. We begin to think to ourselves "are they not like others, or are others not like them"? We begin to see behaviors and traits that are foreign to us. There literally seems to be no way to comfort these children. The screaming fits, lack of eye contact, and incessant need for things to be the same becomes the order of the day. When did they change, and slip into this being that is now unrecognizable?! Why are these meltdowns so frequent and so severe in their intensity?

These nagging questions which are initially relegated to the back of our minds, soon become an over-arching clarion call to search for anyone that can provide a reason for this seemingly sudden and strange behavior. Indeed we try everything known to man to try and handle these behaviors on our own. Sadly, it is to no avail. Not only do we fail at these attempts, we become acutely aware that this crisis is so much bigger than our limited expertise.

After the realization sets in that this "issue" requires outside attention, worry starts to inundate our minds. Ultimately, we make an appointment with the prescribed medical professionals, and we wait. Finally, after anxiously anticipating to hear that it's nothing major; nothing that time and a little speech therapy won't cure. We hear the dreaded words "You're child has Autism Spectrum Disorder". These six words have the power to indelibly mark and change lives! These words are both haunting and piercing. These are the words that no parent desires to hear. The amount of anguish, fear, confusion, and dismay that this diagnosis evokes, completely defies description! What does Autism even mean?! Usually at the moment of diagnosis we are not very savvy on the particulars of Autism, but its reputation precedes it. We may not be well versed on this disorder at the moment of diagnosis, but the purported negative connotations are enough to elicit the feelings of foreboding and panic.

Over the years, many families have been blindsided by the slap of the invisible hand of Autism. And sorely many still are. So many afflicted families are at a loss as to why their family has been dealt this seemingly unfair hand of cards. Many question how they are to precede from here. The painful and intrinsic message of the heart, feels as though the moment that diagnosis was given that our child was officially lost to us. It feels as though they will ever be near yet so far away. What can be done to bridge this gap? And how can it be bridged with Autistic children who are unaware that such a gap exists? And what must we as parents of ASD children do to fill the enormous hole that Autism has left in our hearts?

Subsequent to diagnosis, we are given a list of services that could potentially aid in the care of our Autistic child. When we receive this list there is a quiet confidence that maybe "one of these" will be the shot in the arm to be the catalyst to help "fix" our child. So with eager anticipation and diligence we pursue the therapies route. And thankfully many of the services and the professionals that work them are absolute blessings from Heaven! However, the Autism still remains. The feeling of ineptitude still remains. And the remaining chasm that it created is still a very real and formidable foe. While thankfully there are services available to those that are afflicted with Autism, what are the options that are available for the parent or caregiver?

It is one thing to diagnose an illness or condition, but can there be diagnoses for the unseen emotional and spiritual bondage that it brings? Can this bondage be fixed simply by acknowledging that it exist? How can it be acknowledged when few know that it exists or what to even call it?! The parents/caregivers of the Autistic child soon find that they are engaged in their own battle. The litany of fears, hurt and unidentified emotions are overwhelming to say the least. Many parents feel as if they are swimming in a litany of emotional upheaval and they can scarcely see how to navigate their way out of it. For the parent/caregiver it is indeed life changing!

On an airplane one of the well-known rules is that in case of an emergency landing, all mothers/fathers who are flying with children should first secure their own oxygen masks, and then turn and help the children who are flying with them. The importance of this rule is that clearly the mother/father would be unable to assist their own children in an airplane emergency if they themselves become too injured or impaired. So it is imperative that the parent must first insure their own well-being that they may THEN be able to insure the well-being of the child that is flying with them. In like manner, so it is with the parents of children with ASD. Until we as parents identify, define, and acknowledge the deep-seeded hurt, anger, and resentment that we harbor towards Autism, we can in no wise fully aid and assist our children on their Autistic journey. Not only will we not be able to assist their journey. We have the potential to become a stumbling block to them while they are on their journey. For indeed if we intrinsically harbor negative feelings/opinions about their diagnosis, will it not reflect in our tone when speaking to them?! Will it not be reflected in our overall attitude towards them? Which inadvertently will affect how they feel about themselves. No one is inferring that parents shouldn't have feelings about their child having a diagnosis of Autism Spectrum Disorder, on the contrary, it is very much expected that there will be a plethora of emotions and opinions with regard to it. The danger lies in the parent being oblivious to the aforementioned. It is imperative that the parent/caregiver become acutely aware of their feelings towards the diagnosis of Autism. So important is this awareness that this entire book will be dedicated to the many issues that lie resident in the heart.

For many, it is an all too scary issue to even entertain what could be hidden in the deep recesses of the heart. Some of these attitudes and beliefs are the very lenses through which we view our Autistic children. If we are afraid to even touch these issues how can we see clearly to touch that which concerns our child's autism? May we all take a deep breath and muster up the courage to confront the deeply hidden truths that have guided our every life decisions every step of our way. May we purify and refine that which works and is worth keeping. And may we expose and confront and hopefully annihilate even the most seemingly benign of negative feelings about our children's Autism diagnosis. While this may seem to be a daunting task, and for many it is just that, it is well worth it. For not only will we deal with issues that have been hidden deep in the heart, in many cases, for years. But we will remove the hindrance to seeing the beauty that Autism was meant to bring. Yes, there is a gift that lies hidden within each and EVERY Autistic child. The question is, has our vision been restored to the point that WE may readily see it?!

Chapter 3

Innocent until Proven Guilty

After the crushing blow of the autism diagnosis comes there is an unspoken charge to keep a stiff upper lip and keep it moving. But how? When one receives some of the most devastating news that one could receive about their child and their well-being, how does one just go on with life as usual? Life isn't the "usual "any more. Our whole world has been indelibly marked, and thus changed. This change in part, has do with our view of our Autistic child. Sometimes we receive the diagnosis of Autism but our heads and hearts have not caught up to the revelation that we've received. We haven't intrinsically absorbed the notion that maybe we won't be able to parent this child in the same way as our other children. Our parenting tactics now, must be adjusted.

Regretfully, no child comes with a parenting manual at birth. We as parents are forced to grope and feel our way through the darkness of parenthood. We stumble along our way, and sometimes we repeatedly stumble. At some point we begin to get our bearings and we sort of learn how to navigate parenting a little better.

When we hear the news that our child has been stricken with Autism we are FORCED to recalibrate. There is now an unspoken mandate to begin the groping and the stumbling all over again to learn how to rear this child. The same techniques and devices do not always work for children with Autism. There is indeed a frustration in learning how to parent children with ASD, because typically our inclination is to refer back to the techniques that we already know. The frustration comes when what we would typically do fails to work with our ASD child. These failings can sometimes create not only frustration, but anger and even resentment. We become angry with our child and at our inability to get this child to comply with our wishes. We began feeling disenfranchised by our own child, and thus resentful towards the ASD child, because they are not obeying our commands. But, if we were to do a little soul searching we would probably find that frustration and resentment are not at the root of our discontentment. At the heart of the matter lies fear. Fear itself is a powerful and ominous foe. For when it grips our hearts it causes us to act and react in ways that are uncharacteristic. It causes us to act in haste and in desperation. It is the catalyst for the frustration that we feel. Simply put we fear that which we are unable to control, because the true fear is the fear of the loss of control. Our ASD children become the impetus for facing the fear of the loss of control. When they will not comply, then we feel out of control. When they comply, we feel as if we are in control. This incessant need to be in control is not caused by our children's Autism, but rather it is magnified BY Autism. In the same way that the common cold is not CAUSED by the runny nose and cough that it produces, no, it is caused by a virus. The cough and runny nose are merely symptoms that manifest the virus that was already there. So too it is with our fear of the loss of control. Autism didn't create that feeling. It simply magnifies that which was ALREADY there.

In the same regard, we must be willing to address the issues of anxiety that we face on a daily basis. Many ASD children are wrought with anxiousness. They are not at peace on a day to day basis. Because their world is stimuli based, it stands to reason that it doesn't take much to disturb their peace and tranquility. The slightest of lights, touch, or sounds can cause them to become over-stimulated, and thus over anxious. These anxiety disturbances in many cases will cause them to act out and meltdown. We as their caregivers are then forced to DAILY traverse the hidden landmines of ASD meltdowns. Which in turn builds an anxiety in the caregiver. And rightfully so, for indeed it is nerve-wracking to feel as if we are tethered to a daily emotional land mind. Not knowing which step will cause a meltdown to erupt is indeed unnerving to say the least. So we as parents wake up every morning bracing ourselves for the emotional fall-out of ASD. This over time will begin to create a feeling of fear in the form of dread which will then exhibit itself in the form of anxiety in us. Our anxiety then rears its ugly head when we are forced to encounter the anxiety in our children. This perpetual merry-go-round is the mountain that ASD parents are forced to face. However, if we will take a moment to do some careful introspection, we will see that we have felt these feelings before. Maybe to a lesser degree, but nonetheless, before. Autism is not the first time that we have encountered feeling anxious or nervous. We've experienced anxiety/nervousness at a job interview, or when having to confront someone to discuss a difficult issue. We've most definitely experienced it on our wedding day. So clearly anxiety isn't a fabrication of Autism, but rather Autism mirrors or reflects that which is already there. Autism is the shovel that excavates the heart of the caregiver. It digs up and exposes the issues that lie in repose in the heart of mankind. And for this we are to be grateful. For how can we be delivered from those hidden things, unless they are dug up and brought to the surface?

The resentment of ASD is as pervasive as the disorder itself. For how could we not resent something that has seemingly stolen the "normality" out of our children?! How could we not resent that which intruded upon our plans and our life as a whole? And how could we not resent that which seemingly brings out the worst in us as parents of ASD children? This feeling of resentment, however, is a feeling that is difficult to pinpoint. Often times we blame ourselves for our children's Autism. That blames causes us to believe that we must never show any disappointment or resentment. Thus we walk around blaming ourselves and underneath it all we are resentful about it. We are beholden to the fact that our babies have this awful disorder, so how could we as "good" parents ever feel any resentment towards the victim? But that is precisely how some people feel. We so resent the Autism in them. And for some it inadvertently causes them to resent their child. Now many are not aware of these innate feelings. Nor are they purposely hiding that fact. For many ASD parents they are not aware that they are harboring any type of resentment at all. But in our daily interactions with our children, the spirit of resentment can be readily seen. Again, Autism is not the creator of the roots of bitterness and resentment that some have. It is only the messenger bringing the message. Autism is the letter sent to us by our creator to alert us to that which has taken up residence in our hearts. Most assuredly, we had resentment in our hearts about one thing or another long before we had ASD to be resentful about. What were the origins of this resentment? When did it first inundate our souls? Was it when were children? Or after a bout with unrequited love? Perhaps it was after our parent divorced, and we were forced to reconvene our family in a different way. In any event, resentment was here long before we resented the Autism in our loved ones.

So if we're completely honest we know that Autism is not the fault of the victim. For no one wakes up one morning and says that they will choose today to be afflicted by Autism. We know this….in our heads. But alas, our hearts have yet to receive this inescapable truth. Our hearts in fact fight this truth. Our hearts abhor this truth. Our hearts fear this being true, and thus resents the notion that it must not only be acknowledged but received as a permanent fixture in our lives. We didn't choose Autism, Autism was chosen for us! The problem is that we sometimes resent the fact that we didn't get a "say" in the matter. For if we had a say in the matter we undoubtedly would not have chosen ASD. But ASD has chosen us. In a later chapter it will be made abundantly clear as to why we were chosen, and why if we embrace this careful handmade selection we as well as our ASD children will greatly benefit from the gift that Autism has to bring.

But for now we must deal with the foreboding guilt that we encounter on a regular basis. There is no shortage of guilt to be had by the average parent of an ASD child. From the moment of diagnosis we feel guilty. Did we cause this? Was it the milk they drank? Was it something handed down biologically? Shouldn't we have seen the signs earlier? What were the signs? The list could go on and on. There is an intrinsic need to place blame somewhere, anywhere. And why is there a need to place blame? Why does it NEED to be anyone's fault? Why can't it simply be the way that life is? For many it cannot be this way, because the deep aching of guilt will not allow it to be. The spirit of guilt left unchecked, over time will eat away at us. We even will get to the point where we will feel guilty about things that are not in our control. For instance, let's say you're out in public with your ASD child. All of a sudden that child becomes overstimulated and begins to have a meltdown. But not only do they have a meltdown, they have the mother of all meltdowns. It's in a public place, so quite naturally people begin to stare. Not only do they stare, but they stare with a look of disdain and judgement.

Does not the parent of the ASD child instantly begin to feel ashamed, humiliated, and thus guilty for not being able to control their ASD child? Parents of "typical" children feel this way as well. But with the parent of an ASD child, the guilt of the child's behavior is compounded by the guilt of their child having Autism. On two separate fronts the parent has rendered the decree that they are guilty on all accounts. These perpetual feelings of guilt lead to feelings of shame and shame when left unchecked will lead to feelings of unworthiness. And Unworthiness if left unchecked will begin to create the feelings of hopelessness and despair. And hopelessness and despair often for many leads to depression. But once again, if we can begin to see these epiphanies not as assaults against our character, but rather tools that are sent to sharpen character, then we will not be destroyed by them, but rather strengthened by them. We did not cause their Autism! We were not the creator of it, nor can we eradicate it. But we can become purveyors of the notion that Autism is a blessing in disguise. Once the stigmatism of guilt, shame, fear, etc. has been removed from our mental and spiritual rolodex, we will be able to champion the role that Autism will play in freeing us from the matters that plague our hearts.

Quite naturally we as parents will not be perfect in our endeavors, however, what we can do is choose within our hearts to not harbor negative feelings about our child's Autism, without confronting those issues. The issues most certainly will arise, the question is how do react when they do? Will we labor to identify, and acknowledge those deeply rooted problems? Or will we continue to ignore them, thus allowing fear to hinder the way to freedom? In essence, we have to rescue our hearts from its captivity. The captors are the feelings of anger, frustration, resentment etc. These hidden feelings have taken our heart hostage, and the slightest disturbance will cause these things to reveal their hiding place. Autism is the knight and shining armor that rides in to save the day by revealing our captivity to us. It is one thing to be a prisoner, it is entirely another to be imprisoned, but believe oneself to be free.

Guilt is one of our biggest adversaries. As long as we feel guilty about our children and their Autism we will never walk in the freedom that Autism can provide. We are not guilty. But rather, we have been chosen to be set free, and Autism is the catalyst that will help secure our freedom.

Chapter 4

Picking up the Shattered Pieces

So we've been diagnosed, our world has been shattered by this diagnosis, so where do we go from here? Picking up the pieces can indeed be an arduous and difficult task. It requires a perseverance and determination that must be summoned up from the depths of our soul. We are blindsided by this disorder, we usually are unfamiliar with it and its' inner workings, and we often have nothing in our personal experience to compare it to. For some, you'll have the blessing of a physician who is extremely well versed on Autism, and if they aren't they know just the right person/people to point you to. For some parents of ASD children this is not the case. Perhaps they live in an area where excellent medical care is not an option, hence they are not "schooled" on what approach to take to their children's Autism. Hopefully, with some of the recent findings of increase in Autism, there will be more programs offered, regardless of economic status. It is of the utmost importance that our diagnosed children get early intervention services. The earlier the better. There are various therapies that will be instrumental in the cognitive development of our children. If we research, hopefully we will find a litany of them. Physical, Occupational, and speech therapies are a staple for the newly diagnosed ASD child, to name a few. Consult your pediatrician for a more exhaustive list.

Notwithstanding the physical approach to Autism, there is a psychological approach that is equally as important. This approach for most is not always dealt with on a clinical basis. Usually we don't readily see the portion of the mind that is affected by Autism. For some it is not until much later that we see the mental illness, seizures, or anxiety disorders that may accompany ASD. This in and of itself can be a double whammy! Because in some cases one disorder may mask the other. So medical assessment is integral to the overall health of our ASD children. A primary care physician should absolutely know the appropriate developmental specialist to point us to. From there, there are usually various state sponsored agencies that can assist with coordinated services such as vouchers, tablets (for those ASD children who are speech impaired) and even respite care to name a few. At any rate, these therapies/services ought to be sought with all diligence.

For the Parents of Autistic children the solution is not quite as simple, and not always readily available. For how can we as parents seek help if we can't pinpoint what the core issues are? Without a doubt hands down respite care (care for the ASD child, whether from a professional or loved one to provide families a break in extended care of an ASD individual) is a vital component to the average ASD family. Many ASD families are not aware that such services exist, and thus haven't been able to take advantage of them. But they do exist, and it is important for the welfare of the ASD family to utilize these services. We sometimes don't realize the toll that Autism has on the physical health of the caregiver. Because these affects are latent in nature, their manifestation comes in the form of chronic fatigue, illness, or just an overall malady of the entire being. Again, if we as caregivers are not in good health, how can we provide for our ASD child?

In like manner, what is the condition of our mental health? Surely, being blindsided by the diagnosis of Autism has had a profound effect on our overall being. The amount of stress alone has the potential to wreak havoc on every organ system in our bodies. We must pay careful attention to how our bodies are reacting to this enormous amount of tension. It is deemed stressful because the onslaught of it is unrelenting. This should in no wise be taken lightly. Stress hormones such as Adrenaline are meant to be your body's response to danger, it also increases the heart rate. It is meant to kick in when there is perceived stress or danger. For the ASD caregiver this hormone will be turned on more often then it probably should, which in turn can cause an abundance of issues. Stress is purportedly the catalyst for many health issues such as ulcers, hair loss, high blood pressure and heart attacks to name a few. We must manage our stress levels with all due diligence. For not only does it affect our physical health, it affects the interactions that we have with our children. Undoubtedly, whether they verbally convey it or not they can detect our stress! And it affects their stress levels as well. Which in turn becomes a powder keg for their meltdowns. If we are unable to manage our stress levels how can we teach them how to manage theirs?

The overall wellbeing of the caregiver can't be emphasized enough. For you are the foundation for your Autistic child and the family as a whole. The mental health of the caregiver is equally as important. Our mental health has the potential to set the overall tone for our entire household. For some, Autism takes a greater toll on the mind than it does the body. For we as parents tend to worry incessantly about our children. When we add disability, we increase the level of worry and tension. Although this diagnosis brings with it its' burdens to bare, it also brings with it blessings. We must search for these blessings with a fine tooth comb. Searching to put things into perspective will be instrumental in keeping our stress levels in check.

Although stress and worry are huge factors, hopelessness and despair are equally so. There is for some an unspoken despair that one feels after receiving such a diagnosis. The feeling of a crushing blow comes to mind. Our hearts literally become filled with tears! This was not the plans that we had for our unborn child. We feel as if someone has snatched the rug out from under us, and it causes us to try to scramble to our feet to get our bearings. For some the feeling of sadness is literally overwhelming! We look at our children and wonder what they are thinking and feeling and would they be able to communicate it, even if they knew. The sinking feeling that can fill our mind and hearts when we see their peers frolicking and playing, indeed leaves us wrapped in a melancholy fog. Will our babies one day be able to play with their peers with such abandon? Will we as their parents be able to relax and allow them to? Thankfully, the resilient nature of children allows there to be a resounding answer of yes to all of these questions.

We parents must begin to see our Autistic children, not as Autistic, but simply as children. For indeed every child has a niche in the way that they function and learn. Our children in that sense, are no different than any other child. We just have to search and find out what that niche is pertaining to each individual. Really if we think about it, do we as "normal" people all learn and perceive things in the same way? No, we don't, our approach to life as a race of people is as varied as the colors in a box of crayons. The question is why do we so need things and people to be the same? Is it not the height of arrogance to believe that we are so great that everyone ought to desire to be just like us? If we were to travel through an open field are not our senses exhilarated when we see a field that is filled with an array of wildflowers? Most definitely it is. This perhaps may be partly due to the fact that intrinsically our inner spirit desires to be expanded and challenged by those things that are the unfamiliar. If we desire to evolve and grow as people, then it stands to reason that that growth would not transpire if we never expand our horizons. In the same way, our ASD children come to expand and stretch our horizons. They come to challenge the status quo in us that believes that life should ALWAYS be neatly wrapped and packaged. They dare to redefine "normal" and its negative connotations. They evoke the desire to live outside of the box. And not only do they challenge us to live outside of the box, they question the innate desire in mankind to dare think of "the box" as a symbol of normality and security. So it seems that it would behoove us as caregivers to not so much seek to integrate them into our normality, but rather we should seek to redefine what "normal" is. Is normal having a herd mentality and cookie cutter paradigms? Or is it possible that normal is each individual finding their niche and developing that niche to its fullest potential?! When we develop into our fullest potential, we undoubtedly affect those around us, and when we affect those around us, it challenges their "normal". When their "normal" is challenged it begins to form a rhythm, which in turn can cause mankind to form a symphony, which was orchestrated by the redefining of Autism. May we incline our ears to hear the melody that Autism sings!

And may we as parents of ASD children labor to find what "normal" works for our Autistic children and our families as a whole. This will patently, vary from household to household. What may work for one ASD family may not work for another. It is indeed a case by case endeavor. Again the beauty of it is in the individuality in it. Feel no shame because you can't get your ASD child to do what other Autistic children are doing. Remember, your child will be the litmus test for what works best. Sometimes there may not be anyone else that that particular method will work for. But if it works for your household, then it is to be deemed your new normal. Rest in that knowing that if all musical cords were the same, where would the sense of melody be?! Allow your own research and trial and error to determine what tones you set in your home. As you settle into a pattern of knowing what works and what doesn't you will begin to discover the beauty in the uniqueness that Autism creates. For indeed whether we are conscience of it or not, our soul longs for the opportunity for individual expression. This can be easily identified as we watch our ASD children effortlessly express who they are. It is only when we labor to conform them to the norm that we see a disturbance in the force. By all means, there are certain rules and norms that all must adhere to, and we as caregivers have a charge to try with every ounce of our being to find a unique way to teach our children to adhere to those laws. However, we also have a responsibility to foster an environment whereby they can walk in the truth of who they are, for in this we are enlightened and educated. By doing this we'll discover that the inherent norm in us is challenged. We will begin to question is Autism a curse or a blessing. Ultimately we'll feel a need to question, are they really disabled or is our inability to be free indeed our own disability?!

In any event, this is the road that caregivers will inevitably travel. How often do we meander through life, not necessarily pleased with our life, but nonetheless we accept our circumstances as our lot in life. Often we feel helpless to change it; we wouldn't even know where to begin. As ASD parents, start with Autism. Resign in your heart to not allow Autism to define your child, however do use THEIR Autism as a plumb line to measure and gauge your definition of normal. Allow it to challenge your constructed paradigms. Use it sift through the strongholds of the mind. Allow it, if you dare, to conduct your life's symphony and become the music of the heart.

Chapter 5

Divide and Conquer: The effects of Autism on Marriage

There is not one marriage on the face of this earth that has not withstood some battering storms. Marriage is indeed one of our Heavenly Father's most beautiful gifts! While being a tremendous blessing it has the potential to be both a complicated and a cumbersome affair. We work tirelessly to develop a natural ebb and flow in our marriages and in or homes. This often comes through painstakingly trying various things to find what works. However, once we find what works we tend to hold on to it, white knuckled. For most this formula, more or less will work for them until "death due them part". We usually don't foresee the "suddenly" in life that sneaks upon us and that has the potential to alter our whole world. For really, who looks for those or even dares to prepare for them?!

For many, marriage will inevitably lead to children. We often have our plans laid out in full! And rightfully so, for they are for many, the proverbial icing on the cake. But when we plan for children and one or more of them is stricken with Autism, it is as if our world comes to a screeching halt. We are then forced to find a way to assimilate this unforeseen "suddenly" into our life's plan. Without the proper tools to do so, this addendum to our plan can present a daunting feeling to say the least. We can sometimes perceive that our homes will change because of Autism. But seldom do we count the cost of how it will greatly affect our marriage. More often than not Autism comes into the sanctity of marriage as a stealth bomber. We never saw it coming! We weren't prepared for the toll that it would take. Thus, we are left wondering how to put back together the carnage that it sometimes leaves behind.

Purportedly, the incidence of divorce among married couples with autistic children is astoundingly high! The percentages range is anywhere between 40-64%. Regardless of the numbers we know that the divorce rate is far higher than it should be. This is an unspoken indicator of the profound effect that ASD has on the average marriage. The stress that it adds to marriage defies description. Marriage can be stressful without the component of ASD, but with ASD it is doubly so. There is a tendency for ASD to cause division between the two parents. This in part may be due to the fact that married couples firstly, blame themselves, and then they turn and blame each other. One parent is deemed to be too lenient, the other parent is deemed to be too strict. This lack of agreement causes conflict. For there to be an agreement in ANY contract there must be either two yes's or to no's. Without it there can in no wise be a contract. Often ASD parents, once again, try to rear their Autistic child based on the rules that they knew. When those old rules fail to perform the parents feel frustration, anger, and hopelessness. These feelings begin to concentrate in the parent until one of them begins to question their role as a parent, and thus their role in the marriage. Again the day in and day out stressors of ASD offer no consolation of peace and tranquility.

For some this constant barrage of stress and strife begins to be too much. Like the ASD child the parent(s) becomes over-stimulated and feels that the only recourse is to remove themselves from this seemingly volatile situation. While in the midst of the chaos, divorce may seem like the only viable solution, this however is not the case. Parenting ASD children, or any disabled child for that matter, may be the hardest thing that you may have to face, but it can be done.

The first thing that we have to do is acknowledge that we need to acquire new parenting tools for our children. If we research we will find an abundance of literature on parenting ASD/ disabled children. We'll have to tinker around with this new found information for a while to find what fits our family's needs. Secondly, Parents have to resign in their hearts that divorce is nowhere on the negotiating table. It cannot be seen as an option. If we take it off of the table as an option, then we as married couples are compelled to find another way to confront the issues that plague our marriage and our home. Thirdly, respite care will be a life saver to many. We sometimes are very guarded with our Children, so much so that we dare not trust them into the hands of others. This resolution ties our hands and tethers our marriage to a momentum that can't be sustained indefinitely. We as married couples need a break from the huge responsibility of our children. We need time on a regular basis to recommit ourselves to the promises that we made before our Heavenly Father.

Marriage is truly a beautiful thing. There is no comparison to it. It is indeed special in its' own right. Its' very survival is hinged on the fact that we view it as the precious gem that it is intended to be. We mustn't see it as anything less than that. Marriage is the intertwining of two beings. Each bringing their own harmony. The goal is to skillfully blend the two so not as to destroy the individual rhythm, but instead create a new harmony. That harmony can only function as each person holds to their part that enhances the harmony, and relinquishes the part that destroys it. Autism has not come so as to destroy the harmony between husband and wife, but rather it has come that marriage may be strengthened by it. As we develop a "never say die" mentality in our marriage, we'll begin to see that we must decide how to view Autism's role in our marriage. Since divorce will be deemed as not an option, we'll be obliged to redefine the purpose of the challenge of Autism. Hence, if divorce is not an option, then it would stand to reason that the role of Autism can't be one of dividing and conquering. But rather it must be considered that it is a disguised blessing that is meant to forge in our hearts the character of perseverance. We must strive to parent these children, while simultaneously modeling for them a loving relationship. For many Autistic children are echolalic in their makeup, i.e. they will mimic what they see. If we present a loving and stable environment in the form of a solid marriage then they will know nothing else. They will by their very nature replicate what they have seen. This again is the blessing of Autism, for if we strive for excellence in our marriage, we not only set the right example by living it in front of them, our marriage becomes fortified because of the great effort made to model love before them. How beautiful are the "suddenlies" in our life. Hopefully each time we encounter them we will resist them less and less. As we do so we will not only not avoid them, but we'll begin to search for them in every arena of life. We will do so with an undaunted resolve knowing the treasure that is within the gift of Autism is well worth fighting for.

Chapter 6

Acceptance: Seeing Autism Through the eyes of Truth

The heart of mankind is complex. It is sometimes very difficult to know what another person may really be feeling. Sometimes it's difficult to know what we ourselves are feeling. When dealing with the many facets of disability it is imperative that we know the attitudes of our heart. There are three ways that one is able to see. Firstly, we may see with our natural eyes, secondly, we may see with our minds eye (envisioning something in our mind) or one can see through the eyes of the heart. It is the sight that involves the eyes of the heart that we are most concerned with. For it is through THESE eyes that we view our ASD child, and the diagnosis of Autism. Often times our past beliefs and ideologies color and shape our present and future views. If we had a predisposition toward something in our past it will most assuredly color the lenses of our future. And so it is with the way that we view our Autistic children. Our past hurts and unresolved issues can become a launching point for our opinions about our child's disability. It is not abnormal for the average person to believe that if something has not been an issue for them in their adult life, then it is no longer an issue; Out of sight out of mind. But in reality, this is not usually the case. Those past hurts and pains are still very much with us, thus they lie dormant like a land mind. The moment something or someone steps near those uncharted territories, we instantly react, sometimes to our own surprise.

Our childhood is our foundation. Many of our core beliefs were formed in the earlier years of our development. Hence, depending on what those beliefs were, they will later manifest in our adult decision making. So it would stand to reason that if we had a fairly well rounded upbringing, then we usually to tend to be well rounded as adults. In like manner if our upbringing was more tumultuous as a child that instability can display itself in our temperament as an adult. For example, when we come across an individual that was very quick tempered as a child, unless they have learned how to manage that temper, we will see that that individual is more often than not a quick tempered adult. This disposition has had time to cultivate itself and become a core belief in the individual. If it has become a core belief, i.e. a way that we approach unwanted circumstances, then it would stand to reason that this same mind set will rear its head when that person interacts with their disabled child. In most cases it is not purposeful that a person loses their temper with their child. Nonetheless, it does happen. Usually when a person feels anxious and overwhelmed; there is then a propensity for a loss of temper. So why is anger the go to emotion? Well for many when they try to accomplish what they had in mind, and that accomplishment fails, there is a feeling of anxiety and desperation that takes over. It is in that moment that many will resort to anger, because for many anger is power. We believe that if our first request didn't procure for us the desired result, perhaps intimidation and threatening will. Again for many this is not a conscience decision. This type of belief system has usually been ingrained in the person from a young age. More likely than not that individual watched someone in their family or that they knew, react in the same way. And not only did they react in that way, their angry action garnered for them their intended desire. So now that person learns that anger is a tool that one may use, when all else fails. Again, not intentional, but it is seen as a tool. So it would stand to reason that if our disabled child is out of control, and that meltdown in turn evokes an out of control feeling in the caregiver, then undoubtedly, that caregiver, in a moment of desperation will respond in anger, thinking that their anger is the only way to regain control of the situation.

Alas, for many this destructive cycle can go on indefinitely. And if it goes on indefinitely, it creates a pattern of behavior that becomes very difficult to break. However, for our children's sake it MUST be broken. There are numerous avenues that one may take to seek help for this behavior. There is clinical counseling, anger management, or even churches that offer assistance in these areas. For many going outside of their known circle is an unnerving thought, for many fear what a stranger would do with their most intimate of thoughts. IF that is the case then at the very least prayerfully seek books/workbooks on this topic, there are an inexhaustible amount of them out there. But we have an unspoken mandate as parents/caregivers to address every destructive issue in our hearts that plagues us. We as caregivers deserve to be whole and filled with joy and peace. For many the hurts that you have endured in your own lives has been tremendous. The question is, are you willing to pray for the courage to confront those issues that have kept you tethered to a mindset that isn't who you REALLY are?! Our children will look to us for the template of how to navigate adulthood. Their disability enables us to see our own emotional disability. For these issues can only arise if they're already resident within us. Their challenges come to highlight our own. Their disability enables us, some for the first time, to see our inability to cope with the nuances of life. It allows us to discover hidden strongholds in our thinking that is not only damaging to our children, but toxic to us. It is if the utmost importance that we address the issues that are hidden in our hearts. For the issues are the lenses through which we view our loved one. Sometimes through the cloudiness of our lenses we see these children from a jaded point of view.

We see them as imprisoned; locked away in a world that they are unable to free themselves from. But if we are paying careful attention, we will notice that they are unencumbered. Rest assured that the most profoundly Autistic/disabled child though he/she may seem imprisoned, is in truth, the most liberated. Why? Theirs is a freedom that one cannot procure simply by desiring it to be. Their freedom is inherent, it is innate; their freedom is deeply intertwined with their disability. The gift of their disability allows them to be untethered to the superficial. IT frees them from the fleshly desires of this world. It liberates them from believing that they must hurt or offend in order to advance themselves. It gives them the daily escape from the worries of life. It gives them a greater knowing of that which is unseen. It garners for them the priceless gift of envisioning the world through the eyes of the heart. The gift that they possess quietly nudges our hearts to desire the same freedom that seems to come so naturally to them.

This freedom can be readily had by anyone who truly desires to be free. We have a GPS in the form of our children's disability that points us to the roadblocks to our freedom. When we are dealing with our children and anger, impatience, or irritability manifests itself, these are the unseen roadblocks that Autism alerts us to. The challenge however, is that usually when these roadblocks appear, instead of the caregiver seeing them for what they are, we are instead distracted by the actions of our children. We deem their actions to be the show-stopper of the show. When in actuality their actions are merely promptings to pay attention to what is rising up in us in response to their behavior. Again we can only feel these emotions if the root already lies resident within. And how shall we know of these roots within, but for the interactions with our children on a daily basis?! Maybe we're afraid to look so deeply. Perhaps we'd find at the core of our fears that our child's inability mirrors a helplessness that we would never desire to see or know within ourselves. And yet they are our offspring, so in truth how much of their inability came from us? These are the unspoken fears that hinder the way to freedom. Again, are they REALLY helpless? Or is their helplessness really freedom and strength that is cloaked in an enigma? Look again, very closely at these precious gems. What do you see? Do you see love? Do you see wide eyed wonder? Do you see someone chained longing to get out? OR, do you see a more evolved version of wisdom. One that isn't predicated on pretentiousness, or selfish ambition. DO you see IN them the hope that one day you'll be free?!

A note to caregivers that are outside of the home: teachers, nurses, daycare workers, etc. Yours is a very unique position. For in many cases you get the privilege of encountering, not just one facet of the Autism spectrum, but many. Over the span of your career, you will come across an array of Autistic /disabled individuals. This clarion call to use the navigational tools of Autism is extended to you as well. For if indeed they have crossed your path, then it stands to reason that there are nuggets of wisdom and enlightenment that are just waiting to be discovered by you; providing you are open to receive them. Our Heavenly Father hand selects those who will be enriched by such an encounter. Although at times we may feel the weight of our circumstances, Our Heavenly Father will never give us more than we can bare. Sadly most of us have herd of the horror stories of caregivers that are unkind and actually go as far as to abuse these precious children. They missed the mark. For if they had stopped to observe their child, they would have gleaned from them the very same blessings spoken of in this book. What a travesty to know one of these children, and yet never know them. How tragic to have wisdom stare you in the eyes, but have not the eyes to return its' gaze. And how forlornly, must they look at us and long to see that we are fluent in the language that they speak, so for many they must wait. They must wait for us to recognize what is intrinsic to them. They wait for us to interpret their indescribable beauty. They wait for us to love in a way that will add deeper meaning to loves interpretation. For all of these hopes, they wait.

Chapter 7

The Eyes of an Eagle: Pin Pointing Traits of Autism

Autism is also known as ASD which is an acronym that stands for Autism Spectrum Disorder. There cannot be enough emphasis on the "spectrum" portion of this acronym. For truthfully that is what Autism is: there is literally a spectrum or range for the symptoms of Autism. And they vary from person to person. Not only that these symptoms may sometimes differ depending on the gender. Nonetheless, it is very important that we as parents / caregivers recognize some of the signs of Autism. It is important to note that not every child will have the same symptoms. Some children will have very prevalent symptoms while others may have traits that are much milder which causes their symptoms to be barely detected by the average person. Still it is imperative that we at least be able to recognize a few of the most common traits. If we can recognize some of the defining characteristics of this disorder, then we will be more likely to be able to accommodate them when these symptoms manifest. Again, this is not an exhaustive list of their symptoms, only some of the more noticeable traits.

One of the most familiar symptoms for Autistic children is the meltdowns that some frequently have. These "tantrums" can range in severity and in length. They can have a marked origin or seemingly come out of nowhere. They can last for a minute or two or they can last for a considerably longer span of time. In some cases they will end as abruptly as they began. Because these meltdowns can occur at the drop of a dime it helpful if ASD caregivers really observe and pay careful attention to what are the triggers for these meltdowns. As we become acquainted with the natural ebb and flow of our child(s) personality, we should be able to begin to recognize what things trigger their outbursts. If we can get working knowledge of what triggers their behavior, then we can hopefully divert their tantrum by intervening to extinguish it before it reaches its plateau. For some children when their meltdown is at the onset they can actually be redirected simply by introducing some other subject or toy or book. For some children, depending on their age, they may be able to discuss their frustrations, and may find relief simply by talking about it. For others, deep breathing may help with the overstimulation that they are feeling in that moment. As mentioned before, what triggers these meltdowns varies greatly from individual to individual. It is important that we truly observe our children's personalities and behavior, for these observations will train us to know when they are approaching an outburst, and hopefully these observations will help us to develop a go to plan ahead of time to curtail the impact of this behavior. It is vitally important that learn their cues and become proactive before they get out of hand.

    The topic of the causes of stress and anxiety are almost as broad as ASD itself. Many of those that have been diagnosed with Autism battle with stress and anxiety. Again the triggers for these stressors are a pervasive as the condition itself. Nonetheless, it is an ongoing concern in many ASD households. Because they have sensory issues, then it would stand to reason that it wouldn't take much to overwhelm their senses thus making them feel bogged down with stress. We as care givers must observe our children and begin over time to pinpoint some of the factors that lead up to their stressors. If we sit quietly and observe them, no talking, to redirection, just observation; we can sometimes actually see the "pot" starting to bubble. In other words we can sometimes visually see when they will start to become overwhelmed. For some their meltdowns will actually begin at this point. Much like when we put our children on an eating schedule, we don't necessarily need them to tell us that they need to eat. We know if they had breakfast at 7:30am then it would stand to reason that around snack/lunch time they will need to eat. In like manner if we are observant of their ways we can come to know when their triggers for stress or anxiety are starting to rise. For some they will start to become easily irritated, for others they may begin to wring their hands or flap them. Still others will become irritable in their behavior and speech. Sometimes they may even appear angry, but it may actually be anxiety. Suppose if you will, that you clinch your two fists as tight as you can, we sometimes see toddlers do this when upset. But clinch your two fists as tight as you can, and do that for 5-10 seconds. That feeling that you're experiencing is similar to how their stress and anxiety feels when they are being overwhelmed by it. So you can imagine, if we were to add the component of an angry and impatient caregiver to the mix, our child would be literally inundated with stress and the feelings of being over-stimulated would ensue! We must manage our temper and stress in order to be able the help them manage theirs.

    Sometimes we actually think that they are being defiant, when in actuality, what we are seeing is the manifestation of stress and anxiety. Now, that is not to say that they can't be stubborn or belligerent, for most assuredly some of them are. But we must study carefully to know our child in order to differentiate between the two. And purpose in our minds and hearts to create a battle plan that will hopefully garner for us an environment that is conducive to balance and peacefulness. It can't be stressed enough that yelling is not a proper disciplining tool. Generally when we yell we are deceived into believing that we are gaining control over the situation by exerting power in the form of raising our voice. But in actuality what is really happening is we have lost our power by losing our own self-control. This is counter-productive, because by losing our temper and yelling, we have relinquished our power and yielded it to the situation at hand. It is also counter-productive because the echolalic nature in many ASD children will learn this negative behavior and then add it to reinforce their arsenal of meltdown weaponry. As long as we can begin to learn and recognize their triggers we undoubtedly can stay ahead of the game.

> Echolalia is the repetition of another person's words. With ASD many children have this symptom. They literally "parrot" the speech of their families, or friends or even things that they have heard on television. For some the

majority of their conversations may be echolalic in nature. That is to say they derive very little of their own conversation. They acquire a large portion of their conversation from the "things" that they hear us say. So for example, if you have a household where there's a lot of talk about sports, then you'll tend to hear the ASD child echo some of those same words. If there is a household where a lot of swearing and profanity, then you'll hear that reverberated in your children; particularly when they are upset. So in that sense echolalia can be both curse and blessing. A blessing if we are mindful of the things that they are exposed to; thus ensuring that what they echo is appropriate. And a curse, because if they are allowed to be exposed to things that are negative/damaging, then most assuredly they will mimic those things. We as their parents must become their filter so speak.

There are various symptoms of ASD. Some are finicky eaters, some walk on their toes. Some chew on their clothing, while others must have a regimented schedule without variation. Some don't hear you right away when you call them, and some don't speak at all! Many of them have a specialized area of interest; that thing that they simply can't live without doing. This can be in the form of toys, books, movies or their favorite food to eat. Some don't walk very well, nor do they see well. Some have hardly any visible symptoms at all, and thus are deemed to have Asperger's Syndrome. Whatever the case may be they are so very priceless and precious. Again this is by no means an all-encompassing list. Much research is needed on the part of the caregivers in order to get a better grasp on this disorder. It can only further enhance our understanding, and further undergird our relationship with our child. It is well worth it to become savvy in the blessed tools that Autism can bring.

Chapter 8

To Discipline or Not to Discipline

There has been much controversy over the subject of disciplining children. Parents differ in their opinions of how to discipline and when it is appropriate to do so. This debate will probably continue long into the future, for no one method is a broad brush that can be painted across the face of all children as a whole. But as with all things in life there must be a balance of both love and discipline. We as disciplinarians must make sure however, that we do not chasten our children from the position of our past hurts and disappointments. Our past is much too heavy a burden for them to bare. No, we must rid ourselves of the echoes of hurt; anger, bitterness and rejection that sometimes leave residue in our hearts and on our spirits. This proverbial residue has the potential to line the thoughts and attitudes of the heart and causes us to discipline our children through those lenses.

In all things we as parents must first remove the impairment from our vision before we can even begin to guide them in the way that they should go. This calls for some in depth soul searching on our part. We must go back, in some cases, all the way back to childhood and question; where did I first learn that yelling was appropriate?! Did I hear swearing when I heard yelling? Was there any physically threatening behavior that followed the yelling and the swearing?! If so, how did you feel as a child, hearing and seeing someone tower over you while displaying this sort of behavior? These are the issues that must be delved into before we can choose the most appropriate discipline for our children. For we must never visit upon them unknowingly or otherwise the feelings of unworthiness and rejection that come from this type of discipline. No one is blaming anyone, for most people only do the things that they know how to do. Thankfully, there are many resources to now aid in helping to determine what works best for each household. But we can't allow personal feelings to enter into our chastening method. We mustn't think that giving dirty looks when they do something wrong will shame them into obeying. For the dirty look will only breed unworthiness which will only inadvertently make them act out to get attention so that they will feel worthy; do we see how this is counter-productive?

The same goes for threatening our children; this only creates an environment of fear based relationship. When children grow up in a fearful setting, it leads to them being anxious, and insecure about themselves. It teaches them to have trust issues, and why wouldn't they?! If the people that they should be able to trust most threaten their security and peace of mind, how can they then trust anyone outside of their home? They will most certainly not. Not only that they will develop a resentment and animosity toward their caregivers, that will intern cause them to rebel against almost anything that they are told to do. Moreover, this mindset of rebelling against authority will carry over to their teachers, and thus all authority. And all because we did not set the right tone through the way that we interact with them. Instead of yelling to get their attention, try speaking softly. The more upset they are, the softer you speak. This usually causes them to have to quiet down just to hear what you are saying. Not that this is a miracle pill that will work for every circumstance, but it is a good place to start. Never give up searching for what will work best for your home.

Another tactic that caregivers use often, is they bribe their children. Understandably, some parents have tried everything that they know to do, and to no avail. Out of a last resort sense of desperation they will offer bribes to their child in hopes that it will help them to gain control of the situation. Bribing is "I will give you what you want, if you give me what I want" sort of thing. This particular method is used a lot, even with the best of parenting skills, because it's the method that renders the quickest results. Again the average ASD child is regimented, and hence once these habits are formed with them they can be very hard to break. It forms a pattern and it gets to the point where bribing will seem like the only viable solution. It is not. Rewarding them can be perfectly well and good, however if it is possible, make them earn it. Purchase or even create a colorful chore chart, complete with all kinds of colorful stickers and embellishments. Set up the chart whereby they have to perform certain tasks, and when they do them have a grab bag of items that they can choose from. This will not only stop the bribing game, it will teach them how to wait for things. It teaches them a sense of accomplishment by working for something and earning a reward for it. Lastly, and most importantly it causes a role reversal whereby we are not beholden to our children, i.e. they are not calling the shots. We are their parents, and that seat of authority belongs to us. Thus, we mustn't relinquish that role by allowing ourselves to be controlled by their bribes. In the end we will see that intrinsically they do in an unspoken way cry out for structure and discipline.

When some children are angry or having a meltdown, we as parents try to discipline them at the height of their emotional outbursts. And that is usually the absolute WRONG time to discipline. If they are in the full throws of a meltdown, try the various calming techniques that are available such as soft instrumental music (Christian soaking music works wonders for some), brushing, squeezing a rubber ball, or doing art. Something as simple as in indoor tent works well for some because at the height of their outburst, when they go into the tent, it shuts off the outside stimuli of sights and sounds around them and helps them to get back to center. For some weighted vests provide help as well. There are a litany of products on the market for children/adolescents with ASD.

Once we have hopefully gotten our child to calm down, then we can address their behavior and possibly use something such as the goal chart to further reinforce them working toward a goal of changing their behavior. Reward them when they demonstrate even the tiniest of change. In this way, they will hopefully learn to calm down and then attempt to address their issues. They will also see that they do have the ability to control themselves. Which will in turn will equip them with a skillset that they will carry with them into adulthood. The goal here is to teach the caregiver that we too do not have to be overtaken by the aspects of our child's Autism. We can master the lessons that Autism has come to teach. For no master is a master until he can truly teach his student to become a master.

It is good for our children to know that they have boundaries. In the everyday hustle and bustle of life, there will be rules, laws, and thus limitations. Our children need for their own wellbeing to become familiar with the notion that somewhere in their life (more often than not) they WILL hear the word "NO". They will not only hear it, but they must learn how to be ok with it. Doesn't mean that they have to like it, but they must get accustomed to there being boundaries in their life. Boundaries can be good. Discipline, providing it's done correctly can be good. Even hearing "NO" sometimes can be good. For when we can teach them about reward as well as discipline, we can help to fine tune the character that is already in them. And help them to prepare for the world that lies ahead.

For those ASD children that are able to do homework, even homework can be used as a tool to incorporate discipline in their lives. For many, their regimented nature can facilitate the homework process. If we begin when they are young teaching them to have a regular schedule for homework, then for many they will adhere to that schedule. It may be difficult at first to get them to sit down and do it, but stick with it. Given time and repetition they will learn to adjust. And they will come to expect this to be a part of their repertoire. Note that on some occasions we may encounter resistance from our children with regard to doing their homework. Sometimes it's not a matter of them being lazy and just not wanting to do their assignments. For some homework can be a very frustrating affair. For many they feel overwhelmed and anxious when they don't understand how to carry out their assignment. It is important to note that many of our children do not receive information well by auditory means. Trying to listen to what is being said and comprehending that same information can be truly overstimulating. Because many people, not just ASD people learn better by visual means, it would benefit our children if we can incorporate visual aids while helping them with their homework.

Instead of having them to look at a paper and figure out how to add numbers, try literally putting something such as two apples, crayons, or pencils in front of them. Use visual aids to help their minds to comprehend what is being said. If they visually see it they will be able to receive and translate it better. This by the way can be done for different subjects, not just those subjects that are mathematical in nature. If at all possible have a container with visual aids for each topic that they study already on hand. You may have to assist them with this for the first times, but hopefully they will adapt and know that this is a "helping" container and they will eventually go there on their own for assistance. When they get to the point that their assignments are complete, reward them. This will become a motivator for future assignments.

Discipline should never be used to punish our children. It should be used as a guide to correct incorrect behavior. Therefore, since the goal is to bring about correction, while still keeping their well-being intact, it would stand to reason that we must choose carefully and thoughtfully our modes of discipline. We must prayerfully research based on the temperament and personality of our child what will work best. It will be both trial and error, but eventually we will find something that works. Again whatever we choose it must be balanced with love. We must ensure at all costs that we do not discipline out of anger, frustration, or impatience. For this will only damage our child. We must always calm ourselves first, take a deep breath and realize that just as we don't always know the appropriate thing to do, they do not always know. It is our duty to pilot them through the obstacle courses of life. And not just direct them through life, but skillfully teach them the subtle gradations of it, that what is not innate to them because of their Autism, will be cultivated in them as we together traverse the paths that are trodden by the footsteps of Autism.

Chapter 9

The Sum of All Fears

Oh, how many are the fears that are harbored in the heart of the parents of disabled children. The sleepless nights and worried filled days sadly becomes the norm for many parents. The unanswered question of what are we to do? How shall we raise this child/children without forehand knowledge? How shall we lead them through the stages of life, when life to them means something very different?! How can we plan for their future when ASD doesn't allow one to know what their future may hold? And do we dare tell them WHY their existence is different: why their world is colored differently? How do we as ones who love them so dearly, one day let them go? How?

This journey of parenting disabled children is and will be one of the most challenging and exhilarating things that we will ever do. For indeed, to touch it is to awaken the sleeping heart. To see their Autism we must first see ourselves through their eyes. When they look at us, what do they see? Do we invade their world with our expectations? Do they feel put upon by our frustrations? Or do they feel imprisoned by OUR fears? What they see is made manifest in their faces. Though they may not verbalize what they see and feel, their spirit does. The non-tangible part of them records their interactions with us. And those recordings relay messages to them, messages that we don't hear. These messages have great potential to fill in the gaps of their soul, and thus define who they are.

When we feel the most out of control, we can rest assured that fear is the culprit. We fear for their health, safety, and overall well-being. We even become fearful when they do not fear. Many ASD children are not stranger wary. This can often times be seen in girls with Autism. That fight or flight sense doesn't seem to kick in as readily as it should. Hence they are not as standoffish as we would like them to be. This can produce a hyper-vigilance in the parent to overcompensate for the precaution that the ASD child may not have. By all means we must fill in the gaps for them. We must insert those tidbits of knowledge and wisdom that does not come natural to them. But we must be ever so careful not to fill in their gaps with the fears that plague our hearts. Some of the fears that we hold have nothing to do with our child's disability. Some of those fears have been dormant in our hearts for the majority of our lives. If we search our hearts and ponder these things we'll probably find that Autism was not the liaison between us and our fears. Autism was simply the microscope that magnifies what was already there. When we fear for our babies, inadvertently, it is WE that are fearful.

Fear indeed is a formidable foe, but it most certainly can be defeated. But how can we defeat that which we cannot see? And how can we see that which we so vehemently deny? The wind cannot be seen. But its effects can be felt. Fear cannot be touched with our bare hands, but one can readily see the effects of it.

We mustn't deny that for many it has made contribution to our beliefs and ideas. And now we can see it implementing it policies within the interactions of our children. We must break this cycle. We must look deeply at our own fears. Notwithstanding Autism, what is it that we fear? If we were to sit down and make a list going all the way back to childhood, we would be surprised at the fact that our childhood fears haven't changed a whole lot, they've just perfected what they were going to be. Maybe now you aren't afraid of being hit by a car like you were as a child, but perhaps the fear is that your child will be. Fear lies dormant in the heart, and it waits for something to latch onto so that it can become grounded and firmly rooted in the heart of the person. Then what happens is that anytime a situation arises that closely resembles that original thought of fear, fear then seizes that opportunity to produce fear in you. Once the fear is produced in you it will look for ways to produce those same feelings of fear about the ones we hold so dear. We then unknowingly project those fears onto our loved ones through our fearful interactions with them. In some cases, our children will then pick up and begin to mimic those same fears. Autism mirrors this hidden foe for us. It becomes the barometer that indicates to us that something is unbalanced.

It is of the utmost importance that we learn how to plug into our emotions. That we develop the skills to recognize what is rising up in our hearts. But recognition is only the beginning of the process. We must learn how to be still for a time and truly sit with our feelings and emotions. For many this can cause one to feel an uneasiness, for these are the very feelings that many long to run from. But we haven't we ran from them long enough? Don't you long to be free?! Alas, we long to be free. We are afraid to be a prisoner of fear, but too terrified to be set free. At some point the only way to be freed is to strongly desire to be free. We have to desire it more than anything else. And our motivation for it must be for freedom's sake. There must be an awakening in our hearts that quietly speaks to us and says that liberty awaits. Freedom is calling you through the spirit of Autism in your child.

Parents of all children long for the best for their child.

When our children are born with a disability, we as caregivers have to shift our thinking to accommodate plans for a new best for our children. This in itself has the potential to terrify the caregiver. Because to try to design future plans for these children calls for us to know them on very deep and profound level. To know them at this level one must have the ability to see deeply. And for one to have the ability to see deeply, one must first be able to see self deeply. For many this is a terrifying thought. Look deeply into your heart what is your worst fear? Is death your worst fear? Or is it living? For many the fear of living is real and very palpable. For it is in this daily mindset that one has to navigate and try to survive. The battle causes the fighter to become weary. And not just weary, but one may sometimes become weary in well doing. This weariness in turn causes a person to dread their life and the duties related to it. This dread is rooted in fear. Understandably, it is not difficult to see why caregivers of the disabled would dread waking up some mornings. Because of the regimented nature of our children, we know that on any given day their meltdowns and overstimulated condition will lend itself to at the very least, a tumultuous day. Who wouldn't dread these kinds of days?

Knowing the aforementioned has the potential to make the caregiver approach their days and life in general with a sense of foreboding. We then unknowingly approach our children with this same spirit of disquiet. We have to take a proactive approach to silence the "voice" of dread and angst that councils our inner thought and beliefs. That our inner life may be one wrought in joy and reflect an inner sanctum: one that is laden with an emotional stability that will readily be identified by our children as they behold the face of freedom.

Why is it so important to confront this fear? Imagine waking up every day dreading your life. Literally lying in bed and contemplating the awful existence that you think is your life. If this is how the day begins, it sets the tone for the entire day, and thus becomes the theme for your life. The umbrella of this type of feeling can become difficult to get from under. Indeed we may learn how to exist in this state, perhaps indefinitely, but is existing the same thing as truly living? One can meander through life just barely existing, or we can aggressively pursue that which seeks to deplete our livelihood. Fear zaps our strength; it kills that joy in us that was meant to flourish. Our childhood fears coupled with fears about our children becomes a burdensome weight that is too heavy to bare. We then in turn unwittingly place that same load and burden upon the shoulders of our children. How can we then help to plan their futures when our present appears to be so bleak? The face of Autism comes to challenge the face of fear. It comes to put fear in its rightful place; which is underneath our feet. It comes that we who are fearful may know that we have the ability to conquer our fears. For as we vanquish the purported authority of fear; its power will gradually lessen. As its power dwindles our authority to take back our life is increased. As we see these circumstances begin to change in our lives, there will be an unspoken desire to change them within the lives of our children. We change them in the lives of our children by showing them how to sojourn this life without fear. They will be far more compelled to watch what we do as opposed to listening to what we say because as stated before many learn best by visual demonstration.

As Autism brings with it a litany of hidden lessons, so too does fear. Fear brings with it an unspoken message. That message is that we must never fear letting go of fear. Not only must we not fear it, we must get to the place where we loathe its very existence. It is imperative that we see fear for what it is. It is a slave master seeking to put us into a lifetime of bondage. How so? Well, we are a slave to ANYTHING that has mastery over us. Anything that we have given our power to is now master over us, thus we are enslaved by it.

Fear not the lessons of Autism. For Autism comes not that we may fear it, but that we may be shown our fears about it. And not only do we have fears about our child's disability, but we have a legacy of hidden fears. Autism is the gift that has come to count the cost of the sum of our fears; that we may carefully inventory the chambers of the heart that houses these fears. Autism is the key to help unlock the door of our heart. This door has been closed for many years. It has been closed to many people. It is closed even to us. But for the call of the voice of Autism, it will open, provided we expose the fears of the heart: that Autism may be the key that is used to unlock the doors that will open the way to freedom.

As we traverse the terrain of our hearts we will find deeply buried under our fears, the plans hopes and dreams that we have for our children, as well as ourselves. Seeing ourselves through our children's eyes will help us again to regain our own vision. This will help us to use the wisdom that life offers and pair it with the wonderment that resonates through our babies. Their Autism will lead the way. Daily the special gift of Autism will be a sign that points to every heart infirmity that we have. It will specifically point out and highlight how these fears and anxieties color our daily lives. Our frailties that were once obscured, will become visible to us as we start to see that these infractions do not coincide with the joy that freedom can bring. And as we begin to savor the taste of freedom, we will long all the more for liberty to be a constant in our lives. It is at this point that our vision will begin to adjust. It will no longer be clouded by yesterday, but it will be invigorated by a renewed excitement about tomorrow. With Autism leading at the helm.

Chapter 10

A Letter to Dads

Dear Dad,

You have been chosen for a noble task for such a time as this. Your position in your child's life is one of great importance. There is no one that can take your place; not now, not ever. Your strength and ability to intuitively know how to fix things is a blessed gift from God to you. This same ability to be able to fix things, will sometimes be both your greatest asset as well as your greatest thorn. For there will be days when you look into the eyes of your disabled child and the mechanical nature in you will long to fix what is seemingly broken in your child. You will see their hurt and frustrations and you will long to make them right. Just know, DAD, the hurt and frustration that you will see in them comes as a compassionate gift to you. It comes to allow you the opportunity to surrender your natural inclinations to the unnatural. It comes to offer you an opportunity to dig deeper into the well of the heart and draw out the waters of refreshing that only dads' possess. Only dads' have a look that conveys the comfort of security and protection. Dads' have within them the message that true wisdom is sometimes unspoken. You carry a silent message of both sword and shield. This message will begin to wax greater as you, dad conquer each lesson that Autism brings. As you surrender to its' process, you will not only overcome some things but you will be a living letter of how to unlock the great warrior within.

Chapter 11

A Letter to Moms

Dear Mom,

Such beautiful thoughts of you were in the mind of God the day that he created your role. He lovingly imparted his gentleness and kind nature into the core of your very being; that whenever your children look at you they would be reminded of the love of God. He knew you and knew you well. He knew that it would be second nature for you to love. So he fashioned you in a way that would allow you to carry your unborn child close to your heart. And close to your heart, they are. So close that when you found out about their disability it left a hole in your heart. For you would give your life to take away one ounce of their discomfort. But mom, trust God. Know that he has seen your tears and keeps them in a bottle in Heaven. He knows of the concerns regarding your Autistic child. But he sees it differently. He sees the hidden beauty within you; gifts and talents that you know not of. Your child's disability will be the catalyst to break forth the greatness that lies resident within. Do not blame yourself, or anyone for this most splendid of gifts. For Autism shall be your teacher. It will instruct you how to heal the hole in the heart where dreams did live. IT will help you to discover ever greater dreams; dreams that even you didn't know were there. It will fashion in you the beauty of both wisdom and discretion; that you may embody as a living pillar the most beautiful definition of love.

Chapter 12

The Echo of Responsibility

Echolalia is a characteristic of Autism. It is defined as: a condition associated with Autism. People with echolalia repeat noises and phrases that they hear. They may not be able to communicate effectively because they are sometimes hindered when attempting to verbally express their own ideas. This condition often causes ASD children to repeat WHATEVER they hear. They also tend to mimic what they see. This can have both positive and negative connotations. Quite naturally if they mimic positive behaviors, such as reading writing and mathematics, this would be deemed as a benefit of Autism. However, mimicking behaviors becomes an issue when the behaviors are negative or harmful. We have the opportunity fill in the gaps for them. But the question is what are we filling them with?

For many ASD children outbursts and acting out becomes a daily struggle. The problem may become compounded by external influences. Many of our children are frustrated because either they don't understand, or they are frustrated because they aren't understood. In any event their challenges are real. When they are facing these challenges, often times they are forced to draw from the only things that they know. They draw from those ideas and behaviors that have been stored in their memory. Because many ASD children have very keen memories, they tend to have a plethora of files to draw from. If those "options" that are stored in the memory are positive then that is what they will draw from. But what about when they are not?

How we as parents deal with our issues will be reflected in how our children deal with theirs. We must be careful in or outbursts that they may gradually learn to be careful in theirs.

They will most assuredly look to us to model for them self-control and composure. For any parent in the heat of the moment it is easy to forget that little pairs of eyes are watching us. They are observing us in the same way that people watch television. But, not only are they watching us they are mentally recording our responses to stress and the challenges of daily life. They are honing in on the irritation in our voices and the curt remarks that are exchanged when we feel agitated. They are watching. When they are watching they are learning how to assimilate in society. Hence the tools that we give them will determine how they will function in society once they are left to navigate it on their own.

Language development for some ASD children can be very difficult. There are many ASD children who are unable to speak at all. Then there are others that can verbally speak a few key phrases, but that is the extent of their communicative skills. Then there are those that speak fluently without hindrance of any kind. They are blessed to have the gift of speech. As we are. But how sad is it when we hear those ones that are blessed with speech, use their gift of speech in a way that is derogatory? For there are many little ones with ASD that can use expletives like a drunken adult. Their ability to mimic due to their echolalia goes into warp speed when that is the kind of language that they are undated with on a daily basis. These ones sometimes don't know that swearing in school is inappropriate. So, when something in school doesn't work out their way, and they become frustrated, swearing becomes an instant option, for that is what they have heard. This idea of using swearing to communicate frustration can come from a litany of sources. It can come from television, friends, or their parents. In any event it gets introduced to our children's brain and now enters the folder of their mind.

Parents we have an obligation to model for our children appropriate behavior. For if we teach them that swearing is how we are to handle our daily issues, then that is what they will do. Not only that, when they are irritated with us, they will swear at us. For if this is how we have taught them to communicate, why would they think that we as their parents are off limit. Furthermore, why would a job interview be off limit? We can't expect them to pick up on the social etiquette of knowing when swearing should and shouldn't be used. Autism poses challenges in their social interactions. That is to say that because of their Autism, they do not always understand what is socially acceptable and what is not. But we hopefully do know which words are acceptable and which ones aren't. It is our duty to teach them the difference. For the caregiver of disabled children this is an awesome teaching opportunity. We have the chance to bridge the gaps for them. We have an awesome opportunity to supply them with a multitude of vocabulary words that will not only allow them to communicate effectively, but it will also allow them to colorfully express their thoughts and feelings in a way that is positive and productive.

Regretfully, there is much physical abuse in our world. We see it on the news reports almost daily. Sadly some of those homes will harbor disabled children, and they will be the on the receiving end of some of those abuses. Again if we have been reared in a home whereby physical and verbal abuse was demonstrated, then it stands to reason that some may believe this to be a viable option with regards to disciplining our children. But rest assured it is not. We do not have the right to abuse our children simply because we lack the parenting skills to deal with them. Unequivocally, there is NO excuse or justification for abusing a child, any child! Even our own abuse. If you the parent have been a victim of abuse as a child then by all means please seek help for the hurts and wounds that you probably are still carrying. Abuse is painful and it causes a wounded spirit. It can also breed anger and rage in the heart of the victim. Know that if this description fits you that you are not only hurt by these past egregious acts against you, but you may be in danger of acting them out on your disabled child. Abuse is a serious issue, and it must not be taken lightly. You the parent deserve to be set free from the strangle hold of its effects. When you were wounded physically your soul and spirit were wounded as well. You must seek to heal those wounds so that the legacy of the wounded spirit does not continue on into the next generation of your family. You have the power to end its impact on your family. Just think of how you felt when you were being abused. It caused you to feel rejected, ashamed, and unworthy. Think about it for a moment, when you feel as if you have no control over your child, do you then feel out of control? Do you feel as if violence is the only way to get them to comply with your commands? If so please reconsider that line of thinking. Violence will only beget violence. Your children well replicate the violence waged against them. There are many juvenile detention centers that are filled with children; some of them are ASD children. Many are not diagnosed and thus they are labeled as a problem child. They are not at fault, because for many, society as a whole has failed them. They failed to properly diagnose them, and then they failed to get them the help that they needed. And we as parents fail them when we don't take every opportunity to equip them for this vast and confusing world. Our duty is to lead them by example. We mustn't command the very behaviors from them that we ourselves are not willing to adhere to. We have to walk it out in front of them; that they may readily discern the path that they are to take.

We've all encountered someone in line at the DMV or at the grocery store who truly lacks manners. There is nothing more unpleasant than to go to a customer service desk and the person that is employed to work at that desk has a nasty and disgruntled attitude. They were hired to assist the customer in a calm and courteous manner. But what you get in the way of assistance is anything but calm and courteous. We as the customer are instantly put off buy their behavior, and as well we should be for that type of behavior at the very least IS off putting! What causes people to actually believe that this type of behavior is beneficial? Moreover, why would anyone choose to represent themselves in this manner? For many with these issues they seldom realize that they are coming off in this way. And they seldom realize that they are treating their love ones so harshly. How can one be rude without ever realizing it? Because it has become such a way of life for them that they no longer see their behavior, or the effect that it has on those around them. In like manner we are sometimes oblivious to the effect that our past has on our disabled children. This unconscious behavior must no longer stay relegated to the background of our thoughts. For if it does we will never be cognizant of how we are interacting with our loved ones. For ALL children it is important, but for our disabled children especially so. For many do not have a voice. And even if they have a voice, they may not be able to articulate how this behavior makes them feel. Through our relationships with our children they will learn how to have relationships with others. If the foundational interactions with us is dysfunctional, then it stands to reason that it also will be with others that they encounter. For we are laying their foundation. How we build upon that foundation is directly proportionate with the building tools that we already possess. If we don't have in our arsenal the proper tools to build their foundation, how can we then give them that which we do not have? And how can we acquire those tools if we can't admit that we are lacking them?

The bottom line is this: we are responsible for what we teach our children. Whether directly or indirectly, we are responsible. They are a blank canvas and we are their Van Gogh. As parents we have the opportunity to impart greatness or implement stumbling blocks before them. We have opportunities to help mold and shape them into someone extraordinary. They are born with beauty already intrinsic to them. What we contribute to their growth and development either facilitates their growth or it stunts it. We must not be responsible for the latter. They look to us for everything. We are ALL that they have in this world. They desperately need a fighting chance. Please don't allow the hurts of the past to ruin our children's future. Fight to be free that in turn we may be instrumental in their freedom. They have locked away deep inside of them treasures and gifts that are waiting to be opened. We mustn't crush what lives on the inside of them. We must not be resentful of the beautiful gift that their disability brings, instead with all of our hearts we must embrace it. Not only must we embrace it WE need to discover the beauty of the mysteries that it holds. Their disability is the key to unlock the doors to our past feelings of hurts and disappointments. Autism will show us the way. For if we allow it and allow ourselves to surrender to the process, Autism will hollow out the stony parts of the heart, by first allowing them to be seen, and secondly by allowing us to recognize every time they are manifesting themselves.

To walk in integrity is difficult, because it calls for us to choose it time and time again. But if we will resign in our heart to live it daily, then we will set the bar for our children. We will set a standard for them; that even if they come short of meeting that standard they will at least know that the standard exists. But as they watch us struggle daily to meet that standard they will not only know of the set standard, but they will also learn of the challenges that come with it. The struggle itself will be their teacher. For in their attempts to walk in integrity, they will learn through the struggle what works and what does not. The endeavor of seeking to walk upright will provide for them both successes and failures. It is this natural ebb and flow that will procure for them the strength of a persevering character. This strength they will greatly need as they sojourn through this precarious world. But, because they will have their parents as a forerunner they will not falter. For they will have a living example of responsibility that will be echoed by the perseverance that came before them.

Chapter 12

Treasures in Jars of Clay

A treasure is defined as something that is valuable and difficult to replace. There are many things in this world that we esteem. For many they are the treasures that can be seen and felt. Some value education, prestige and yes even money. But somewhere along the journey of life we stumble upon an inescapable truth: that the most priceless things on this earth are the things that cannot be seen. The gifts of enlightenment, understanding, and wisdom are indeed priceless. These most treasured of all possessions cannot be bought or sold. They must be sought after as one would search for gold or silver. We must seek after them not simply for acquisition's sake, but that we may be enriched and strengthened by them. Most importantly that we may have something that is truly esteemed as priceless to offer to our children.

Many families in their wisdom will work tirelessly in their careers that they may amass a wealthy inheritance to leave for their posterity. They painstakingly divide their wealth and store it for safe keeping, so that when they pass on from this life their children will have financial security in their absence. In like manner we as must carefully ponder what legacies will we leave to our children? What tools will our children have waiting for them? In many cases we were left to inherit both blessings and curses from our forefathers. We see this play out on the world stage frequently. How many of us have experienced the kind temperament that grandma possessed while she was still alive and well? Most definitely we can see it, for when we see it manifested in a family member, in that moment we become acutely aware that we are seeing the remnants of her personality being displayed in them. Conversely, we also have seen those who suffer from alcoholism; and the effects that it has on the entire family. Sadly, for some this addiction will be repeated in the family in latter generations. The point, is what will we as parents of the challenged and disabled, leave behind for them. What shall their legacy be? Will we leave behind for them a stable, grounded, and well-rounded personality tools? Or, will we leave them the image of anger, impatience and foul language as their communicative skills? We have the opportunity to leave with them a plethora of communicative skills and tools, but first we must master them ourselves. We must be willing to readily receive and accept the challenge and gift of raising our children. Not only must we be willing to rear them, but we must be willing to rear them in a loving and nurturing environment. We can only provide this type of environment for them if these qualities are innate within in us.

Our Heavenly Father created us with wonderful plans in mind. He carefully placed within us gifts and talents to be able to do and accomplish things that are beyond our imagination. Our children were sent to help us to evolve and grow. What parent doesn't desire to see their child mature?! Our Father in Heaven is no different. HE knows the heights and plateaus that he desires for us to reach. He meticulously designed us with gifts as well as challenges. In his supreme wisdom he knew the circumstances that would stretch us and allow us to grow. We must not strive against his will. Not for his sake, but for ours. For it is always to our benefit when we learn to persevere and overcome. Not only will it behoove us to do so, but there is a beautiful gift of wisdom that is both priceless and eternal. IT cannot be acquired by any other means. We have to experience the ups and downs that life has to offer. We must not only enjoy the pleasurable times, but we must embrace the challenges and disappointments as well. For it is the hurts and disappointments, sufferings and loss that is most instrumental in producing in us the character and integrity that are the marquee of one who has passed through the proverbial fire, and wasn't destroyed in the fire, but rather was refined by it.

The gift of Autism IS that refining fire. Indeed many things are and will be. But for parents both the blessings as well as heartaches of parenting are meant to be our teacher. For some parenting experiences will bring utter exhilaration and joy, and on other days our hearts with writhe with angst and despair. These issues are a juxtaposition that was supremely designed to refine the greatness in us. If we will allow it to. The key here is all in the way that we see it. How we view hardship and calamity, is directly proportionate to the amount of issues that we need to be delivered from. The greater our shunning, the greater the need to be "tried" by these same fires. It is important that we try with every ounce of our being not to be consumed by the challenges, but rather we should seek to glean the wisdom out of them.

Again the treasure that wisdom holds, can be found quite readily under your very own roof. Your children hold some of the keys that will unlock hidden treasure. They are in part a reflection of you. Do you not see it? How beautiful they are, and yet how complex. How filled with hope and creativity and yet they are angry and frustrated. How sometimes they are plagued by fears and in the next moment they are fearless. They've come to show us, ourselves. They also come to reflect our unspoken captivity. And yet, while they are reflections of it, simultaneously they hold the keys to being liberated from it.

> This is the beginning of the journey to discover the meaning of life. Philosophers have laboriously pondered these issues. Perhaps the answer is that it isn't this enigma that everyone thinks it to be. Perhaps the answer is more pragmatic, yet supremely sublime. Maybe one doesn't have to search "out there" for the meaning of life, perhaps we begin the search inwardly. When we search our mind and our hearts, what is it that we see? Do we discover that our foundational beliefs are merely predicated on someone else? Do we REALLY believe that our favorite color is blue, or is blue being our favorite color inferred by someone from our past? What is YOUR inward truth? At the very least do you question what was always deemed to be true? Truth is freedom. It can be unpleasant at first. For many fear and pride won't allow us to see truth, let alone search it out. But the eyes

of our children look at us and demand for the truth to be told. For how can we teach them about truth if we ourselves are offended by it? Truth is not our sworn enemy, it is our deliverer. It comes not to rob or steal, but rather to restore. It comes not to destroy, but to reconstruct what years of hurt and pain has sought to denigrate. Truth comes to mold our hearts; as the potter does his clay. For clay to be molded it must soft and pliable in the potters hand. The question to us as parents, is will we surrender our hearts to this most invasive of processes? Truth much like a surgeon's scalpel, is exacting with its objectives. It is clear cut and concise, for freedom demands it. We can be liberated, but for our liberation to take place, we must resolve in our hearts not to shoot the messenger. We mustn't allow position, prestige, or partiality to dictate our surrender.

We must learn how to ride the wave of truth. If we will become careful students of it, we find that it will begin to benefit us. We will find that it not only will seek to free us, but in doing so it will become a comfort to us. The gift of truth comes already intertwined in our children's disability. Each and every trial related to their disability is given graciously to tug at our hearts and souls. Their disability is our truth meter. For how else would things that are buried so deep cease to remain obscure? Embrace their disability for in so doing you will unknowingly embrace truth, thus facilitating an unspoken invitation to open the way to freedom.

In summation, many are the plans for our disabled children. We love and adore them so very much. So much so that we are devastated at the very thought of their having to suffer. But there is a silver lining to every cloud. They were awesomely created! They are not broken, we are: they've come into the world to fix us. They bring with them a proverbial magnifying glass that allows us to see our frailties for what they really are. These frailties; as unpleasant as they are, aren't meant to garner judgement or criticism. They are there simply as indicators to point to the need to be freed. In this regard even our frailties can be deemed as blessings. For indeed how would we know of the undetected virus without the symptom of a cold? How would we detect the onset of a fire, unless we first smell the smoke? How will we see our brokenness if we believe that we are yet whole? The blessing of discovering the truth through our daily interactions with our disabled children, are indeed treasure in jars of clay. For inherent in their disability is an unwritten map that will lead to our freedom. Much like hidden treasure, one must dig deeply in order to discover it. So too must we make the most of each opportunity with our children, that we may not waste one opportunity to discover the hurts, frustrations, and pains that hinder the way to our freedom. We were created to be free. For in freedom the fullest expression of creativity and beauty are easily seen. We were made not to just have fleeting glimpses of it, but we were fashioned to walk in it daily. Some of us as we begin this sojourn will not only discover our "TRUE" feelings, but we will discover gifts and talents that we didn't now were there. For hurt and pain were blocking them. Ultimately, we will find that it is not only our children who have this awesome gift on the inside of them, but we'll discover that we do as well. We too are earthen jars of clay that contain glorious treasures on the inside of us. There is an awesome beauty contained on the inside of each one of us. Our individuality is a sort of spiritual fingerprint that is unique only to us. No one else has it, and no one can duplicate it. Like fine wine or aged cheese we were meant to improve with age. Our children's challenges are the catalysts that assist with our maturation process. The Heavenly Father is not finished with us yet. For as we continue to live in this world we are commissioned with the unspoken charge to continue to thrive and flourish in it. How sad would to have children yet they never reach adulthood. How disappointed would we be if we planted a seed, but it never grew?! In the same way our evolution as adults must continue until the day that we leave this earth. It was meant to be this way. For is it not a most pleasant of experiences when we encounter someone who has already gone through this process. When we sit with them and converse with them we find they ooze wisdom. We hear that their conversation is seasoned with knowledge and enlightenment. We observe that they possess the power of steadfastness and self-control; for indeed they allow NOTHING to move them. They embody a timeless tale of strength, character, and perseverance which in turn makes them a lovely sight to behold.

We too are called to travel such a journey. In like manner, we will have our turn to be the clay upon the wheel of the potter. As we surrender to the molding of the master's hand, we'll discover that the sum of our parts is so much greater than we realized. Once this realization takes place we will be able to not only walk in this truth, but we'll be able to lead our children on the journey of a lifetime, that will culminate in them reaching their greatest potential.

Treasures in Jars of Clay

We gaze upon their face, and gently we smile
For many are the plans for this newborn child
We think to ourselves, they'll grow up to be
someone great
While carelessly forgetting,
that we are not masters of their fate
We watch as they develop and suddenly
within…….we think
Are they not like others, or are others not like them
A litany of emotions begin to cascade within
We begin to blame ourselves for our past and present sins
An anxious trip to the doctor confirms our greatest fears
Autism has taken captive the ones that we hold dear
Anger and hurt now floods our heart
This child seems so broken, where do we even start
We start at the beginning with the creator of our child
For he is all knowing, and he has known all the while
He has blessed this child with gifts from above
They are made manifest as we learn to walk in love
When we surrender to our Heavenly Father
We will learn a new way
To discover these beautiful treasures
That are hidden in jars of clay

Michelle Coleman

www.ingramcontent.com/pod-product-compliance
Ingram Content Group UK Ltd.
Pitfield, Milton Keynes, MK11 3LW, UK
UKHW041954230426
12048UKWH00008B/330